Parties & Ponies

CHILDREN'S MENU COOKBOOK

recipes & styling

DAWN HARRIS BROWN

photography & design

RACHEL CHOTIN LINCOLN

Browncroft Publishing Company

Published in the United States by Browncroft Publishing Company LLC,
Covington, Louisiana.

www.browncroftpublishing.com

ISBN 978-0-9883496-0-5

Printed in China

Design by Rachel Chotin Lincoln
Photography credits appear on page 86.

10 9 8 7 6 5 4 3 2 1

First Edition

The recipes in this book have been carefully tested by the author. The
publishers and the author have made a good faith effort to ensure that
the recipes and instructions are accurate and safe, but cannot accept
liability for any resulting injury. All recipes should be performed under the
direct supervision of an adult.

CONTENTS

05   BEACH PONIES & SEAHORSES

15   CIRCUS PONY

27   COWPOKES & COWPONIES

37   FIESTA BURROS

47   MAGICAL PONY

55   READ TO MY PONY

65   SLEEP OUT WITH MY PONY

73   TEA TIME WITH MY PONY

Beach Ponies & Seahorses

SHELL PASTA SALAD

FRUIT KABOBS WITH CHOCOLATE DIP

BEACH BALL SPRITZER

SEAHORSE SPRINKLE CAKE

STARFISH FOR MY PONY

Shell Pasta Salad

16 ounces shell pasta
12 ounces frozen steamer vegetables
1 cup grape tomatoes (sliced in half)
1 (6 ounce) jar quartered, marinated artichoke hearts
1/3 cup mayonnaise
salt

1. Cook pasta as directed. Drain, let cool, and place in a medium mixing bowl.

2. Steam vegetables as directed in microwave. Let cool and pour over pasta. Add sliced tomatoes.

3. In a separate bowl, drain artichokes. Add mayonnaise and mix well.

4. Pour drained artichokes over pasta salad and add salt.

5. Pour the mayonnaise mixture over pasta salad and mix well.

serves 8
Suggestions: Serve in small, colorful sand pails with wooden spoons. Shred lettuce in the bottom of each pail, and pile the pasta salad on top.

Fruit Kabobs

pre-cut fruit pieces
wooden skewers
1 pineapple

1. Using a variety of pre-cut fruit pieces (strawberries, cantaloupe, melon, pineapple and grapes), create kabobs by alternating fruit pieces on wooden skewers.

2. Stick the kabobs into a fresh pineapple on a round plate. Serve with Chocolate Dip.

Chocolate Dip

1 cup plain greek yogurt
1/2 cup nutella

Mix yogurt and nutella in a small bowl until smooth. Serve with Fruit Kabobs.

PARTIES & PONIES

Beach Ball Spritzer

3 melons (cantaloupe, watermelon, honeydew)
1 (12 ounce) can frozen limeade concentrate
48 ounces sparkling water
ice

1. Cut melons in half and remove seeds. Scoop out balls using a melon baller. Arrange melon balls on a baking sheet and place in the freezer for an hour.

2. In a pitcher, mix frozen limeade concentrate with sparkling water and add ice.

3. Fill glasses with frozen melon balls and pour limeade spritzer over top.

serves 8

Suggestions: For an added sweet touch, run a lime wedge around each glass and dip in sugar. Garnish with mint and sugar swizzle sticks.

Seahorse Sprinkle Cake

1 purchased pound cake
1 container white icing
sprinkles
seahorse cookie cutter

Cut the pound cake into 1/2 inch thick horizontal slices. Spread a thin layer of icing over the entire slice. Shake sprinkles over the icing. Use a seahorse cookie cutter to cut out the cake pieces.

makes 6

Starfish for My Pony

**1 watermelon
star cookie cutter**

Cut watermelon into 1/2 inch thick slices. Use a star cookie cutter to cut out starfish pieces. Serve to your pony guests and beach kids!

Circus Pony

JUGGLING POPCORN BALLS

JUMP THROUGH A HOOP HOTDOGS

TIGHTROPE ROASTED PEANUTS

RINGMASTER'S APPLE SLICES

PURPLE PONY SMOOTHIE

Juggling Popcorn Balls

6 cups popped popcorn
1/4 cup agave nectar (or honey)
1/4 cup creamy natural peanut butter
1/4 cup dried fruit (chopped)
1/4 cup chocolate chips
coconut

1. Place popped popcorn in a large mixing bowl.

2. In a microwave-safe bowl, microwave agave nectar and peanut butter on high for 1 minute. Stir until smooth. Pour sticky mixture over popcorn.

3. Add dried fruit and chocolate chips. Stir until sticky mixture and toppings are mixed well with the popcorn.

4. Dip clean hands into ice water. Quickly and firmly press the popcorn mixture into 2" balls. Roll balls in coconut and allow to cool. Store wrapped in plastic wrap in airtight containers.

makes 12
Variations: For a stickier consistency, add more agave nectar and peanut butter. Add nuts, chopped ginger, pretzels or coated chocolate candies to the popcorn mixture. Roll balls in chopped nuts, toasted sesame seeds, granola, sprinkles or ground chocolate cookies.

Jump Through A Hoop Hotdogs

12 dinner rolls
12 cocktail sausages
1 red onion (sliced)
mustard

1. Heat sausages according to package directions. Slice dinner rolls lengthwise (only half-way through).

2. Place sausages inside the dinner rolls. Slip hotdogs through onion ring slices and top with mustard or desired condiments.

makes 12

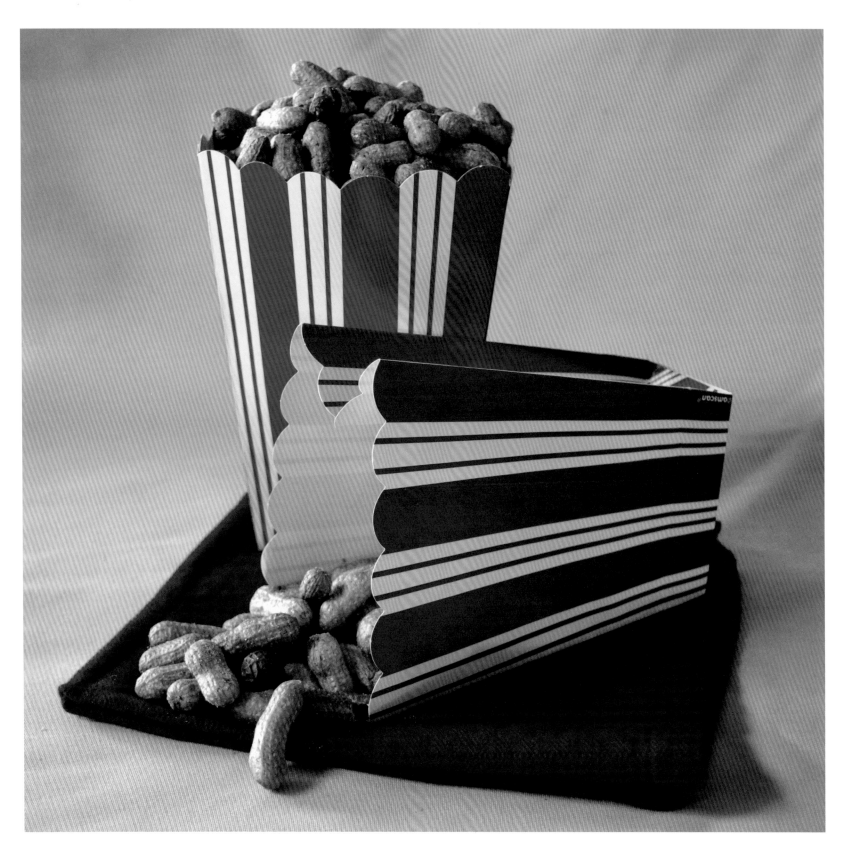

Tightrope Roasted Peanuts

1 pound in-shell raw peanuts
1 teaspoon Cajun seasoning
salt

1. Preheat oven to 350 degrees F.

2. Arrange the peanuts on a large baking sheet lined with parchment paper or foil.

3. Roast for 20-25 minutes on the middle shelf of the oven.

4. Using oven mitts, carefully remove the baking sheet from the oven. Sprinkle Cajun seasoning and salt while the nuts are still hot. Allow to cool a little before eating.

serves 8
Variations: Sprinkle hot peanuts with cinnamon or Parmesan cheese instead of Cajun seasoning.

Ringmaster's Apple Slices

2 large red delicious apples
almond butter
animal crackers

1. Wash, core and slice the apples into 1/2 inch rings.

2. Spread each apple ring with 1 tablespoon of almond butter.

3. Stand animal crackers around the perimeter of the ring.

makes 8
Variations: Try peanut butter, nutella or cream cheese instead of almond butter.

Purple Pony Smoothie

1 cup blueberries
1/2 banana
1 container blueberry yogurt
1 tablespoon honey
1 cup of ice

1. Place all ingredients in a blender.

2. Blend until smooth and purple.

serves 2
Suggestion: Use frozen fruit for an ice cream texture.

Cowpokes & Cowponies

RODEO RANCH POTATO SALAD

BANDANA BAKED BEANS

BRONCO BURGERS

RUNAWAY ROOT BEER FLOAT

Rodeo Ranch Potato Salad

1 pound fingerling potatoes
1/2 cup ranch dressing
1 cup diced celery
salt and pepper

1. Boil fingerling potatoes until tender. Drain and cool. Slice potatoes into bite-sized pieces and place in a large mixing bowl.

2. Pour ranch dressing over the potatoes and add diced celery. Mix well.

3. Add salt and pepper to taste. Stir until combined.

4. Chill and serve.

serves 8

Bandana Baked Beans

4 (15 ounce) cans of ranch beans (or baked beans)
1 red onion
iron skillet
bandana

1. Preheat oven to 350 degrees F.

2. Slice red onion into rings.

3. Place beans in an iron skillet.
Sprinkle the top with onion rings.

4. Bake for 45-60 minutes or until bubbly. Using oven mitts, carefully remove the skillet from the oven and allow to cool.

5. Serve in the iron skillet with a bandana tied on the handle.

serves 8

Bronco Burgers

1 package frozen turkey meatballs (fully cooked)
24 (2-inch) rolls
lettuce
6 small tomatoes
1 red onion
barbeque sauce

1. Warm meatballs in microwave according to package directions.

2. Cut rolls in half horizontally.

3. Tear lettuce into bite-size pieces. Cut tomatoes and onions into thin slices.

4. Place 1 teaspoon of barbeque sauce on the bottom of each roll. Stack lettuce, tomato and onion slices on bottom. Add meatball and secure top half of roll with a toothpick.

makes 24

Runaway Root Beer Float

vanilla ice cream
root beer

1. Place a scoop of vanilla ice cream in a plastic mug.

2. Fill with root beer.

3. Add a big straw, spoon and enjoy!

serves 1

Fiesta Burros

SOMBRERO ORANGE SLICES

FISH, CHICKEN & BEAN TACOS

SOPAPILLA CHEESECAKE

SUGARED TORTILLAS

PONY PIÑA COLADA

Sombrero Orange Slices

6 navel oranges
1/2 cup honey
1 teaspoon cinnamon

Peel and cut oranges into thin slices. Arrange on a round plate. Add cinnamon to honey and stir to combine. Drizzle over oranges.

Fish, Chicken & Bean Tacos

purchased grilled fish or fish sticks
purchased grilled chicken strips
purchased bean dip
shredded cabbage
shredded lettuce
shredded cheese
salsa
ranch dressing
taco shells

1. Heat purchased fish and chicken according to package directions. Cut into small pieces and place in separate serving dishes. Empty bean dip into a serving dish.

2. Arrange lettuce, cabbage, cheese, salsa and ranch dressing in separate bowls.

3. Assemble Fish Tacos: Place fish and cabbage in a taco shell. Top with ranch dressing.

4. Assemble Chicken & Bean Tacos: Place chicken or bean dip in a taco shell. Add lettuce and cheese. Top with salsa.

serves 8
Suggestion: Arrange all ingredients in separate bowls and display as a self-serve taco bar.

Sopapilla Cheesecake

1 can crescent rolls
1 (8 ounce) package cream cheese, softened
1/2 cup sugar + 2 tablespoons for topping
1 teaspoon vanilla
2 tablespoons melted butter
2 teaspoons cinnamon

1. Preheat oven to 350 degrees F. Press 1/2 of the crescent rolls into an 8" x 8" baking pan (or pie pan) sprayed with oil.

2. Mix cream cheese, 1/2 cup sugar and vanilla until smooth. Spread on top of the crescent rolls in the pan. Sprinkle with 1 teaspoon cinnamon.

3. Place the other half of the crescent rolls over the cream cheese mixture. Pour the melted butter over the rolls. Sprinkle the top with remaining sugar and 1 teaspoon cinnamon.

4. Bake for 30 minutes.
Con mucho gusto!

serves 8

Sugared Tortillas

1/4 cup sugar
1 tablespoon cinnamon
8 purchased tostadas (crispy whole corn tortillas)

1. Preheat oven to 400 degrees F.

2. Mix sugar and cinnamon in a small bowl. Place tostados on a baking sheet and sprinkle with cinnamon sugar.

3. Bake for 5 minutes. Let tortillas cool before eating.

makes 8

Pony Piña Colada

1 (14 ounce) can coconut milk
1 (6 ounce) can pineapple juice
2 cups ice
pineapple slices for garnish

Blend all ingredients in a blender until smooth. Garnish with pineapple slices.

serves 4

Magical Pony

AMBROSIA

CUCUMBER CLOUD SANDWICHES

GOSSAMER GRAPES

DREAMY ICE CREAM PIE

Ambrosia

1 can mandarin oranges in light syrup (chilled)
1 cup shredded coconut
2 cups mini-marshmallows

1. Place mandarin oranges (with syrup) in a bowl.

2. Add coconut and marshmallows.

3. Toss all ingredients until well combined and serve.

serves 4

Cucumber Cloud Sandwiches

1 container soft cream cheese
1 English cucumber
salt
1 loaf white whole wheat sandwich bread
flower cookie cutter

1. Spread cream cheese over 2 pieces of bread.

2. Slice the cucumber very thinly and pat dry with a paper towel. Place several slices on the bread, spread with cream cheese. Sprinkle with salt. Place the other cream cheese bread piece on top.

4. Using a flower cookie cutter, cut the sandwich into a cloud. Repeat for all bread slices.

makes 8

Gossamer Grapes

1 bunch green grapes
1 package lime jell-o

Wash the grapes and place a small (damp) cluster in a plastic storage bag. Add jell-o powder and shake until covered. Refrigerate for several hours.

Dreamy Ice Cream Pie

3 tablespoons butter or margarine
1 package marshmallows
6 cups crispy rice cereal
1 (1/2 gallon) container ice cream
sliced fruit, chocolate sauce or caramel sauce

1. Melt butter in a large saucepan over low heat. Add marshmallows and stir until melted. Remove from heat. Pour in rice cereal and mix until well coated.

2. While still warm, press cereal mixture into a greased pie plate for the pie shell. Dip your clean hands in ice water for easy pressing.

3. Fill shell with your favorite ice cream and top with fruit. Keep in the freezer until ready to serve.

serves 8

Variations: Top Ice Cream Pie with chocolate sauce or caramel sauce.

Read to My Pony

MANDARIN ORANGE ICED TEA

PRETZEL PAINT PONIES

KISS MY COLT COOKIES

PALOMINO CHEESE POPS

MY PONY'S PEPPERMINT TREATS

Mandarin Orange Iced Tea

4 cups water
4 mandarin orange herbal tea bags
1 tablespoon honey
1 cup orange juice
2 oranges (sliced)

1. In a saucepan, bring water to a boil. Add tea bags, remove from heat, cover and steep 4-6 minutes. Discard tea bags and stir in honey.

2. In a heat-resistant pitcher add orange juice, orange slices and top with ice. Pour sweetened tea into pitcher and serve.

serves 4

Pretzel Paint Ponies

mini pretzels
rolo candies (unwrapped)
pecan halves

1. Preheat oven to 300 degrees F. Prepare a baking sheet with parchment paper. Arrange pretzels in a single layer and top each with 1 rolo candy. Bake for 4 minutes.

2. Using oven mitts, carefully remove the baking sheet from the oven. While still warm, press a pecan half onto each candy covered pretzel. Cool completely before storing in an airtight container.

PARTIES & PONIES

Kiss My Colt Cookies

1 cup sugar
1 cup creamy peanut butter
1 egg
18 Hershey Chocolate Kisses (unwrapped)

1. Preheat oven to 350 degrees F. Prepare a baking sheet with parchment paper.

2. Mix the sugar, peanut butter and egg together in a bowl.

3. Take a piece of dough (in your clean hands) and roll it into a 1 inch ball or use a small ice cream scoop. Keep forming balls until all the dough is used.

4. Place evenly apart on the baking sheet. Bake for 12 minutes.

5. Using oven mitts, carefully remove the baking sheet from of the oven. While still warm, press an unwrapped kiss in the center of each cookie. Place cookies on a rack to cool.

makes 18

Palomino Cheese Pops

shredded Parmesan cheese
poppy seeds
wooden skewers

1. Preheat oven to 400 degrees F. Prepare a baking sheet with parchment paper.

2. Pile the cheese in a circle spaced evenly apart on the baking sheet. Sprinkle with poppy seeds. Place a wooden skewer in the center of each cheese circle and top with more cheese.

3. Bake for 5 minutes or until the cheese melts. Using oven mitts, carefully remove the baking sheet from the oven and let cool completely in the pan.

4. Carefully lift the cheese pops from the parchment paper and arrange in a flower pot filled with uncooked beans or shelled nuts.

My Pony's Peppermint Treats

2 cups rolled oats
2 cups bran
2 cups (self-rising) corn meal
12 ounces molasses
1 cup dark corn syrup
1 cup (self-rising) flour
1 teaspoon salt
1/4 cup warm water
red and green peppermints (unwrapped)

1. Preheat oven to 350 degrees F. Prepare a baking sheet with parchment paper.

2. Mix all ingredients together, except the peppermints. Roll into 1 inch balls and place on the baking sheet.

3. Bake for 16 minutes or until golden brown. Using oven mitts, carefully remove the baking sheet from the oven. While still warm, press an unwrapped peppermint in the middle of each treat. Allow to cool completely.

makes 24+
Suggestions: Stencil horse designs on burlap, glassine or paper bags. Fill bags with treats and feed to your pony friends!

Sleep Out with My Pony

CARROTS & YOGURT DIP

SADDLEBAG WRAPS

GALLOP GOOEY MARSHMALLOWS

CINNAMON HOT CHOCOLATE

Carrots & Yogurt Dip

1 (16 ounce) bag baby carrots
6 ounces Greek yogurt
1 tablespoon garlic and herb salad dressing mix

Combine yogurt and salad dressing mix in a small bowl.
Refrigerate for 30 minutes for seasonings to blend.
Serve with carrots.

serves 4

Saddlebag Wraps

1 (3.5 ounce) jar pesto sauce
1 cup mayonnaise
1 jar roasted red peppers
2 purchased grilled chicken breasts
shredded cheese
lettuce
4 spinach or sun-dried tomato wraps

1. In a small bowl, mix pesto sauce and mayonnaise.

2. Remove red peppers from the jar and pat dry on a paper towel.

3. Slice chicken and place in small bowl.

4. Assemble wraps: Spread 1 tablespoon of pesto mayonnaise mix on each wrap. Add sliced chicken and 1 roasted red pepper. Top with cheese and lettuce. Roll and tuck sides like a burrito. Secure with toothpicks and cut in half.

makes 4
Suggestion: Place all ingredients in separate bowls and allow guests to create their own wraps.

Gallop Gooey Marshmallows

nutella
chocolate chip cookies
lemon curd
lemon cookies
peach slices
cinnamon waffles
marshmallows

1. Spread nutella on a chocolate chip cookie. Spread lemon curd on a lemon cookie. Place peach slices on a cinnamon waffle.

2. Roast marshmallows until browned and gooey.

3. Top each cookie and waffle with 2 toasted marshmallows and sandwich second cookie or waffle on top.

Cinnamon Hot Chocolate

hot chocolate mix
cinnamon stick
marshmallows

Prepare hot chocolate according to package directions. Stir with cinnamon stick and top with marshmallows.

Tea Time with My Pony

SADDLE UP SCONES

JAM'S TEA CAKES & EASY ICING

PRANCING FLOWER POTS

CINNAMON APPLE TEA

CARROTS & APPLE SLICES

Saddle Up Scones

4 cups flour
1/2 teaspoon salt
1 teaspoon baking soda
3 ounces raisins
1-1/2 to 1-3/4 cups buttermilk

1. Preheat oven to 400 degrees F. Prepare a baking sheet with parchment paper.

2. In a medium bowl, sift the flour, salt and baking soda. Add the raisins.

3. Make a well in the center and pour most of the buttermilk in at once. Using one hand, mix the flour in a circular motion, adding more milk if necessary. (The dough should not be too wet and sticky.) When the dough comes together, turn it out on a well floured surface. Wash and dry your hands.

4. Pat the dough into a 1 inch thick round. Cut into wedges, and bake for 20 minutes or until golden brown.

makes 8-12
Variations: Instead of raisins, add dried fruit, chocolate, nuts or cheese. For added sweetness, add 1/2 cup sugar.

Jam's Tea Cakes

1 cup butter (softened)
2 cups sugar
3 eggs
3 tablespoons milk
1 teaspoon vanilla
5 cups flour

1. Preheat oven to 325 degrees F. Prepare a baking sheet with parchment paper.

2. Using a hand electric mixer, cream butter and sugar in a large mixing bowl. Add eggs one at a time. Add milk and vanilla. Add flour one cup at a time and mix until the dough comes together.

3. Refrigerate dough for 30 minutes or more. Roll out on a floured surface to 1/4 inch thickness and cut with cookie cutters.

4. Place tea cakes on the baking sheet and bake for 12-15 minutes. (Do not overcook, as the cookies will be too hard.) Serve plain or decorate with Easy Icing and sprinkles!

makes 24

Easy Icing

1 cup powdered sugar
2 teaspoons milk
2 teaspoons light corn syrup
1/4 teaspoon almond extract
assorted food coloring

Stir together powdered sugar and milk in a small bowl until smooth. Beat in corn syrup and almond extract until icing is smooth and glossy. If icing is too thick, add more corn syrup. Divide into separate bowls and add food coloring. Dip cookies into icing or paint them with a brush.

8 small clay flower pots
1 purchased pound cake
ice cream (any flavor)
chocolate cookies

Wash and dry the small clay flower pots. Cover the drain hole in the bottom with a piece of cake. Fill with your favorite ice cream. Sprinkle crushed chocolate cookies on top. Push a straw in the middle and place a fresh cut flower. Add a seed packet and spoon with a rubber band and tie with raffia.

Cinnamon Apple Tea

4 cups of water
4 cinnamon apple herbal tea bags
2 tablespoon honey
1 cup unsweetened apple juice (or cider)
cinnamon sticks and apple slices for garnish

1. In a saucepan, bring water to a boil. Add tea bags, remove from heat, cover and steep 4-6 minutes. Discard tea bags.

2. Stir in honey and apple juice. Serve with cinnamon sticks and apple slices.

serves 4

Carrots & Apple Slices

1 (16 ounce) bag baby carrots
2 apples (sliced)

Pile baby carrots and apple slices on a plate. Serve to your pony friends!

Index

A

Agave Nectar, 17
Almond Butter, 22
Ambrosia, 49
Animal Crackers, 22
Apple
    Apple Juice, 81
    Cinnamon Apple Tea, 81
    Carrots & Apple Slices, 81
    Ringmaster's Apple Slices, 22
Artichoke Hearts, 7

B

Banana, *See Fruit*
Bandana Baked Beans, 31
Barbeque Sauce, 33
Beach Ball Spritzer, 11
Beans, 31, 41
Blueberries, *See Fruit*
Bread
    Crescent Rolls, 43
    Dinner Rolls, 19
    Rolls, 33
    Sandwich Bread, 51
Burgers, 33
Butter, 43, 53, 77
Buttermilk, 75

C

Cabbage, 41
Cajun Seasoning, 21
Cake, 12, 79
Candy
    Hershey Chocolate Kisses, 59
    Peppermints, 63
    Rolos, 57
Carrots
    Carrots & Apple Slices, 81
    Carrots & Yogurt Dip, 67
Celery, 29

Cereal, 53
Cheese
    Cream Cheese, 43, 51
    Shredded Cheese, 41, 69
    Parmesan Cheese, 61
Chicken, 41, 69
Chocolate
    Pretzel Paint Ponies, 57
    Kiss My Colt Cookies, 59
    Cinnamon Hot Chocolate, 71
    Chocolate Dip, 9
    Juggling Popcorn Balls, 17
Cinnamon
    Cinnamon Apple Tea, 81
    Cinnamon Hot Chocolate, 71
    Sombrero Orange Slices, 39
    Sopapilla Cheesecake, 43
    Sugared Tortillas, 45
Coconut, 17, 45, 49
Cookies
    Easy Icing, 78
    Gallop Gooey Marshmallows, 71
    Jam's Tea Cakes, 77
    Kiss My Colt Cookies, 59
    My Pony's Peppermint Treats, 63
    Prancing Flower Pots, 79
Cream Cheese, *See Cheese*
Cucumber, 51
Cucumber Cloud Sandwiches, 51

D

Dreamy Ice Cream Pie, 53

F

Fish, 41
Fish, Chicken & Bean Tacos, 41
Fruit
    Apple, *See Apple*
    Banana, 25
    Blueberries, 25

Chocolate Dip, 9
Dreamy Ice Cream Pie, 53
Dried Fruit, 17
Fruit Kabobs, 9
Grapes, 51
Lemon Curd, 71
Melon, 11
Orange, *See Orange*
Peach Slices, 71
Pineapple, 9, 45
Raisins, 75
Watermelon, 11, 13
Fruit Kabobs with Chocolate Dip, 9

G

Gallop Gooey Marshmallows, 71
Gossamer Grapes, 51

H

Honey, 17, 25, 39, 57, 81

I

Ice Cream
    Dreamy Ice Cream Pie, 53
    Prancing Flower Pots, 79
    Runaway Root Beer Float, 35
Icing, 12, 78

J

Jam's Tea Cakes, 77
Jell-O, 51
Juggling Popcorn Balls, 17
Jump Through a Hoop Hotdogs, 19

K

Kiss My Colt Cookies, 59

L

Lemon, *See Fruit*
Lettuce, 41, 69

Limeade, 11

M
Mandarin Orange Iced Tea, 57
Marshmallows
       Ambrosia, 49
       Cinnamon Hot Chocolate, 71
       Dreamy Ice Cream Pie, 53
       Gallop Gooey Marshmallows, 71
Mayonnaise, 7, 69
Mustard, 19
My Pony's Peppermint Treats, 63

N
Nutella, 9, 71

O
Onion, 19, 31
Orange
       Ambrosia, 49
       Mandarin Orange Iced Tea, 57
       Orange Juice, 57
       Sombrero Orange Slices, 39

P
Palomino Cheese Pops, 61
Pasta, 7
Peanuts, 21
Peanut Butter
       Juggling Popcorn Balls, 17
       Kiss My Colt Cookies, 59
Pecan Halves, 57
Peppermints, *See Candy*
Pesto Sauce, 69
Pineapple, *See Fruit*
Pony Piña Colada, 45
Popcorn, 17
Potato, 29
Prancing Flower Pots, 79
Pretzel, 57

Pretzel Paint Ponies, 57
Purple Pony Smoothie, 25

R
Ranch Dressing, 29, 41
Ringmaster's Apple Slices, 22
Roasted Red Peppers, 69
Rodeo Ranch Potato Salad, 29
Rolls, *See Bread*
Root Beer, 35
Runaway Root Beer Float, 35

S
Saddle Up Scones, 75
Saddlebag Wraps, 69
Salsa, 41
Sausage, 19
Seahorse Sprinkle Cake, 12
Shell Pasta Salad, 7
Sombrero Orange Slices, 39
Sopapilla Cheesecake, 43
Sparkling Water, 11
Starfish For My Pony, 13
Sugared Tortillas, 45

T
Taco Shells, 41
Tea
       Cinnamon Apple Tea, 81
       Mandarin Orange Iced Tea, 57
       Jam's Tea Cakes, 77
Tightrope Roasted Peanuts, 21
Tomato, 7, 33
Tostadas (Tortillas), 45
Turkey Meatballs, 33

V
Vanilla, 43, 77, 78
Vegetables, 7

W
Watermelon, *See Fruit*
Waffles, 71
Wooden Skewers, 9, 61
Wraps, 69

Y
Yogurt
       Carrots & Yogurt Dip, 67
       Chocolate Dip, 9
       Purple Pony Smoothie, 25

Conversion Tables

MEASURING LIQUIDS BY VOLUME

TSP.	TBSP.	FLUID OZ.	CUPS	PINTS	QUARTS	GALLONS
3 tsp.	1 tbsp.	1/2 oz.				
	2 tbsp.	1 oz.				
	4 tbsp.	2 oz.	1/4 cup			
	8 tbsp.	4 oz.	1/2 cup			
	16 tbsp.	8 oz.	1 cup			
		16 oz.	2 cups	1 pint		
		32 oz.	4 cups	2 pints	1 quart	
		128 oz.	16 cups	8 pints	4 quarts	1 gallon

VOLUME

U.S.	METRIC
1 tsp.	5 milliliters
1 tbsp.	15 milliliters
1/4 cup	59 milliliters
1 cup	236 milliliters
1 pint	473 milliliters
1 quart	946 milliliters
1 gallon	3.8 liters
METRIC	**U.S.**
10 milliliters	2 tsp.
30 milliliters	1 fluid oz.
100 milliliters	1/2 cup minus 1 tbsp.
500 milliliters	2 cups plus 2 tbsp.
1 liter	4 1/4 cups

MASS

U.S.	METRIC
1 oz.	28.35 grams
1 pound	454 grams (0.45 kilogram)
METRIC	**U.S.**
100 grams	3.5 oz.
500 grams	1.1 lbs. (17.6 oz.)
1 kilogram	2.2 lbs. (35.2 oz.)

ABBREVIATIONS

tsp.	teaspoon
tbsp.	tablespoon
lb.	pound
oz.	ounce

TEMPERATURE

FAHRENHEIT	CELSIUS
32° F	0° C
100° F	37.8° C
212° F	100° C
300° F	148.9° C
350° F	176.7° C
400° F	204.4° C
450° F	232.2° C

Credits & Acknowledgements

BEACH PONIES & SEAHORSES:
Pony: ***Chubby Checkers***, *Carousel Farms, Folsom, LA*
Children: ***Kayleigh****, age 9, Covington, LA;* ***Kylie****, age 7, Loranger, LA;*
Sammy*, age 9, Franklinton, LA;* ***Wyatt****, age 5, Franklinton, LA*

CIRCUS PONY:
Ponies: ***Chubby Checkers*** *&* ***Magic****, Carousel Farms, Folsom, LA*
Children: ***Cali****, age 6, Folsom, LA;* ***Fischer****, age 10, Mandeville, LA;*
Jacobie*, age 5, Covington, LA;* ***Julia****, age 7, Franklinton, LA;* ***Mason****,*
age 12, Folsom, LA

COWPOKES & COWPONIES:
Pony: ***Teddy Bear*** *(Carousel Farms), Marlene & Ray Lieber,*
Mandeville, LA
Children: ***Daylan****, age 9, Covington, LA;* ***Jackson****, age 6, Abita*
Springs, LA; ***Olivia****, age 4, Abita Springs, LA*
Props: ***Spencer's Feed and Seed****, Folsom, LA*

FIESTA BURROS
Donkeys: ***Henry*** *&* ***Poncho****, Lauraine & Hose Wytenus, Folsom LA*
Children: ***Allie****, age 6, Folsom, LA;* ***Daylan****, age 9, Covington, LA;*
Mia*, age 10, Mandeville, LA;* ***Reece****, age 10, Metairie, LA*

MAGICAL PONY:
Pony: ***Magic****, Carousel Farms, Folsom, LA*
Children: ***Olivia****, age 9, Mandeville, LA*

READ TO MY PONY:
Pony: ***Whiskey*** *(Carousel Farms), Bill Johnson, Mandeville, LA*
Children: ***Julia****, age 7, Franklinton, LA*

SLEEP OUT WITH MY PONY
Pony: ***Chubby Checkers****, Carousel Farms, Folsom, LA*
Children: ***Harris****, age 4, Covington, LA;* ***Noah****, age 6, Covington, LA*

TEA TIME WITH MY PONY/FRONT COVER:
Ponies: ***Chubby Checkers****, Carousel Farms, Folsom, LA;* ***Teddy Bear***
(Carousel Farms), Marlene & Ray Lieber, Mandeville, LA
Children: ***Connor****, age 7, Mandeville, LA;* ***Gracie****, age 6, Mandeville,*
LA; ***Jacobie****, age 5, Covington LA;* ***Marissa****, age 7, Mandeville, LA;*
Olivia*, age 4, Abita Springs, LA*

BACK COVER:
Caroline*, New Orleans, LA;* ***Harris****, Savannah, GA;* ***Reid****, Shanghai, China*

ENDSHEETS:
Abba*, Lafayette, LA;* ***Alex****,* ***Bou****,* ***Leah*** *&* ***Luke****, Mandeville, LA;* ***Allie****,*
Folsom, LA; ***Anna****,* ***Caroline*** *&* ***Sam****, New Orleans, LA;* ***Arden*** *&* ***Owen****,*
Novato, CA; ***Barrett****, Folsom, LA;* ***Beau****,* ***Isobel****,* ***Mikaela*** *&* ***Talina****,*
Cooktown, Australia; ***Brooklyn****,* ***Kate*** *&* ***Samantha****, Fishers, IN;* ***Carter***
& ***Skylar****, Covington, LA;* ***David****,* ***Joe*** *&* ***Victoria****, Covington, LA;* ***Daylan****,*
Covington, LA ; ***Elizabeth****, Baton Rouge, LA;* ***Fischer****, Mandeville, LA ;*
Gaja*, San Sebastián, Spain;* ***Gavan*** *&* ***Karley****, Abita Springs, LA ;* ***Hallie****,*
Hank *&* ***Hayes****, Mandeville, LA;* ***Harris****, Savannah, GA;* ***Jackson*** *&* ***Olivia****,*
Abita Springs, LA ; ***Jacobie****, Covington, LA;* ***Joseph****,* ***Mary*** *&* ***Walker****,*
Prattville, AL; ***Julia****, Franklinton, LA;* ***Kaden****,* ***Layla*** *&* ***Mason****, Phoenix,*
AZ; ***Kayleigh****, Covington, LA;* ***Kylie****, Loranger, LA;* ***Liam****, Arlington,*
VA; ***Mackenzie****, Franklinton, LA;* ***Makenna****,* ***Shane*** *&* ***Ty****, Boerne, TX;*
Margaret*, Boerne, TX;* ***Marissa*** *,* ***Mia*** *&* ***Naomi TaoXuan****, Mandeville, LA*
; ***Martha****,* ***Mary*** *&* ***Sarah****, Lexington, KY ;* ***Olivia****, Mandeville, LA ;* ***Olivia****,*
Sydney, Australia; ***Rachel*** *&* ***Hannah****, Covington, LA;* ***Reece****, Metairie,*
LA; ***Reid****, Shanghai, China;* ***Sammy****, Franklinton, LA;* ***Vann****, Baton*
Rouge, LA; ***Wyatt****, Franklinton, LA*

RECIPES:
Hand Model: ***Caroline Schieffelin,*** *New Orleans, LA*
Jam's Tea Cakes: ***Lindsey Voight Richardson's*** *great-grandmother's*
recipe, p 77.
Sopapilla Cheesecake: *Adapted from* ***Chula Homa Hunt*** *Program, p 43.*

PHOTOGRAPHY: *All photographs within the chapters of this book*
were taken by ***Dawn Harris Brown*** *and* ***Rachel Chotin Lincoln*** *(with the*
assistance of ***Rosamary Chotin*** *and* ***J. Scott Chotin, Jr.****) on location*
at ***Carousel Farms*** *and* ***Browncroft Farm****. Photographs of Val:* ***Karen***
Clevley*, p 87.*

The authors of this book would like to thank Bonny Barry for not only
providing the ponies for the photoshoots, but also for her time and
energy spent wrangling both children and horses! Also, a big thank
you to all the children, parents and behind-the-scenes helpers who so
lovingly cooperated in all the photoshoots.

Bonny Barry
CAROUSEL FARMS

Bonny Barry's lifetime love of horses began when she started riding and showing American Saddlebreds at the age of four. From there she went on to train and show Arabians and her life's path was set. Bonny wanted to work with horses and use their special (some would say magical) nature to help people. She received her certification as a therapeutic riding instructor from the Cheff Center and used this to found "Equitation Therapy", a non-profit therapeutic riding program. Bonny also ran the equestrian division of the Special Olympics for four years.

Bonny has participated at Equine Affaire as a part of the celebrity horse showcase with her horse Val representing the Georgian Grande breed. As part of this honor Val had a figurine made in his likeness by Stone Model Horses.

Bonny now teaches students and trains horses using natural horsemanship techniques. In her spare time she enjoys entertaining with her trick horse, Clyde, a Clydesdale that Bonny rescued as a baby and who steals the show and the hearts of all who see him perform.

Bonny trains from her home, Carousel Farms, in Folsom, Louisiana. She has a daughter, Babs Burley, who works as an elementary school teacher.

Boarding • Lessons • Training • Rehabilitation • Transportation

Carousel Farms
Folsom, Louisiana
www.carouselfarms.org

The End